MARK NEVIN

PIANO FOR ADULTS

A COMPLETE COURSE FOR THE OLDER BEGINNER

CHORD AND INTERVAL APPROACH

EDWARD B. Marks Music Company / HAL•LEONARD® CORPORATION

EXCLUSIVELY DISTRIBUTED BY

7777 W. BLUEMOUND RD. P.O. BOX 13819 MILWAUKEE, WI 53213

Purpose of this book

This book is designed for the older beginner at the piano, without reference to age limits. It is intended to fill the need of the student who has never had previous lessons or the student who had lessons in childhood and now requires a "refresher" course. This method is equally suitable for individual or class instruction.

The following important fundamentals are covered in this book:

DIRECTIONAL NOTE READING
INTERVALS
CHORDS and TRIADS
SCALES (Major and Minor)
KEYS and KEY SIGNATURES
FINGER TECHNIQUE

Teaching points are presented through appropriately graded piano compositions by the author, as well as through suitable arrangements from the works of the great masters (Beethoven, Brahms, Mozart, Chopin, Tchaikovsky).

Contents

Naming The Keys

PIANO KEYS ARE NAMED AFTER THE FIRST SEVEN LETTERS OF THE ALPHABET

A - B - C - D - E - F - G

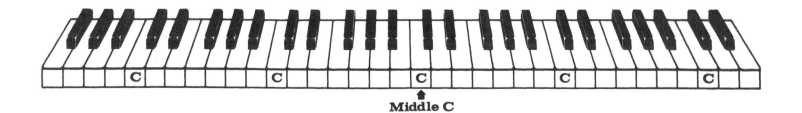

THE BLACK KEYS

It is important to notice that the black keys fall into two groups, either (1) a PAIR (Twosome) or (2) a GROUP-OF-THREE (Threesome). Their names will be discussed later in the book.

TWO LANDMARKS, C and F

You can find any C on the keyboard because it is always located to the left of the PAIR of black keys. You can find any F on the keyboard because it is always located to the left of the THREESOME. Without looking at the keyboard, try to locate each C and each F. You can do this by "feeling" for the Twosome and the Threesome.

The Piano Keyboard

STUDENT: On the keyboard illustration below, write the letter name of each white key.

Middle C

Music Fundamentals

THE STAFF

The Staff consists of 5 lines and 4 spaces.

TREBLE CLEF or G CLEF

TREBLE STAFF

BASS CLEF or F CLEF

BASS STAFF

BAR LINES and MEASURES

The Music Staff is divided into measures by Bar Lines. For example:

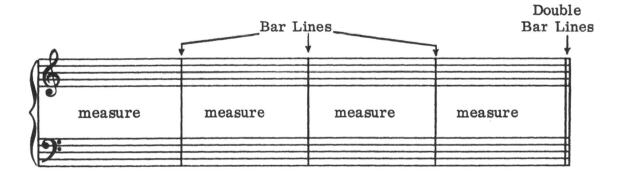

Numbering The Fingers

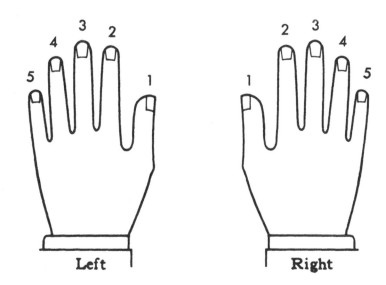

Notes

Notes have time values. The note with the longest time value is the WHOLE NOTE. Learn the following table of time values.

o = WHOLE NOTE, held for 4 counts.

= HALF NOTE, held for 2 counts.

= QUARTER NOTE, held for 1 count.

= EIGHTH NOTE, held for half the time value of a $\frac{1}{4}$ note.

Time Signatures

At the beginning of every music staff there is a TIME SIGNATURE, which consists of 2 numbers, an upper number and a lower.

For example:

Upper number indicates there are 4 counts in each measure.

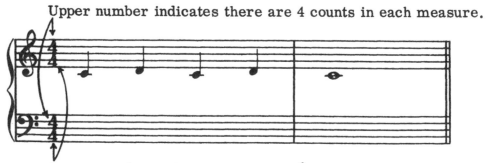

Lower number indicates that each $\frac{1}{4}$ note will receive one count.

Correct Hand Position

A correct hand position at the keyboard requires

  1. Finger-tip contact with the keys
  2. Curved Fingers
  3. Arched Knuckles
  4. Wrist slightly lower than the knuckles

Learn These Notes

The illustration below shows the location of 5 notes (A-B-C-D-E) on the staff, and their corresponding keys. Study them, and learn to locate each on the keyboard. *Observe that the middle C note in the lower staff is the same middle C as shown in the upper staff.*

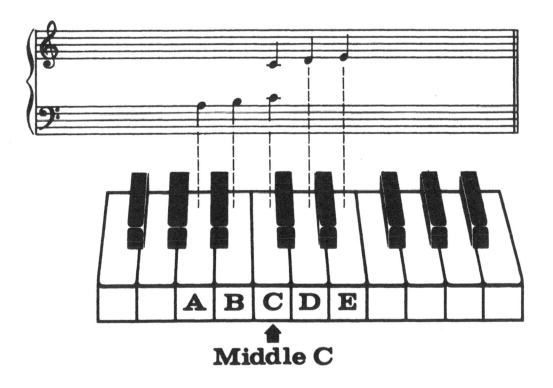

After having learned the 5 notes above, and their correct location on the keyboard, you are ready to play the pieces on the following page.

8

The Interval Of A Second

An INTERVAL is the distance in pitch between any two given tones.

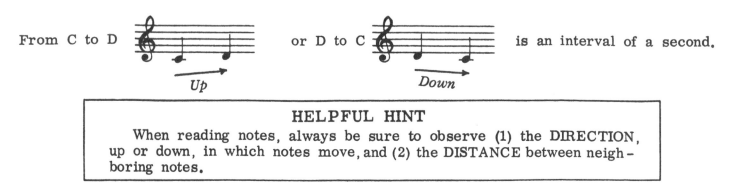

From C to D   or D to C   is an interval of a second.

> **HELPFUL HINT**
> When reading notes, always be sure to observe (1) the DIRECTION, up or down, in which notes move, and (2) the DISTANCE between neighboring notes.

Do, Re, Mi
(A Tune For The Right Hand)

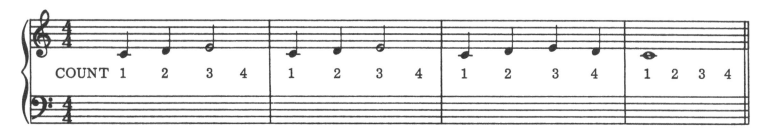

HOW TO PLAY THE ABOVE TUNE

1. Place R.H. 1 (thumb) on Middle C, 2 on D, 3 on E. Then COUNT ALOUD as you play each note. Say or sing — 1-2-3-4 in each measure.
2. Play the tune again, but this time sing or say the syllable names, Do, Re, Mi.
3. Play it again, but this time sing or say the letter names — C, D, E.

IMPORTANT:
Repeat the above procedure, but this time start with R.H. 2 on C, 3 on D, 4 on E. OBSERVE that notes that are next to each other are played by fingers that are next to each other.

Do, Ti, La
(A Tune For The Left Hand)

1. To play the above tune, place L.H. 1 (thumb) on Middle C, 2 on B, 3 on A. Follow the same directions as outlined for playing the R.H. tune above.
2. Repeat this procedure, but this time start with L.H. 2 on C, 3 on B, 4 on A.

New Notes

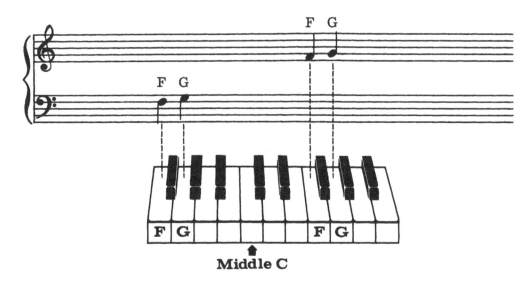

Play each of the following tunes three ways.

    1. By count.

    2. By syllable name.

    3. By letter name.

Five By Five
(A Tune For All Fingers)

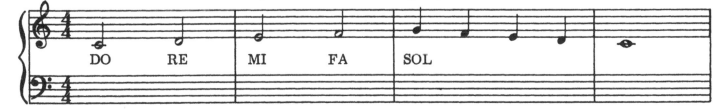

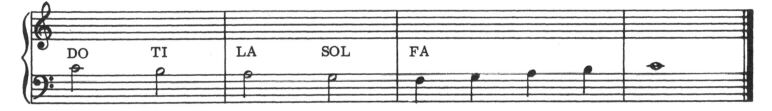

Five By Five
(In A Different Rhythm)

The Interval Of A Third

Notes that are a skip apart are played on white keys that are a skip apart. This is an interval of a third. See illustration below.

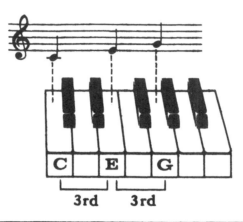

> ### HELPFUL HINT
> Develop the habit of keeping your eyes on the music and not on your hands. Also, be sure to play each note with equal pressure --- especially when the melody shifts from the right to the left hand; keep the melody flowing.

SUGGESTION: The following piece contains examples of intervals of a second and intervals of a third. Find as many as you can of each.

REMINDER: Be sure to COUNT ALOUD.

Theme from the
"Surprise" Symphony

FRANZ JOSEPH HAYDN
1732 - 1809

> ### EXPRESSION MARKS
> **p** stands for "soft", from the Italian word "piano".
>
> **f** stands for "loud", from the Italian word "forte".

The Interval Of A Fourth

There are several examples of the interval of a Fourth in the song "Good King Wenceslas".
Find as many as you can.

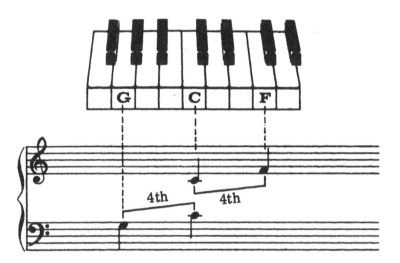

Good King Wenceslas

Traditional Carol

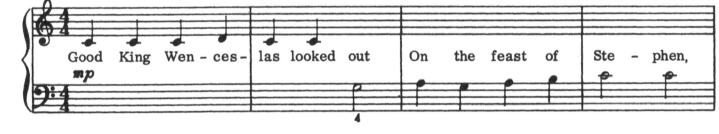

Good King Wen - ces - las looked out On the feast of Ste - phen,

mp

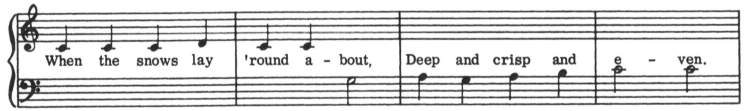

When the snows lay 'round a - bout, Deep and crisp and e - ven.

mf

Bright - ly shone the moon that night, Though the frost was cru - el,

When a poor man came in sight, Gath - 'ring win - ter fu - el.

NEW EXPRESSION MARKS

mp stands for "medium soft", from the Italian words "mezzo piano".

mf stands for "medium loud", from the Italian words "mezzo forte".

New Notes

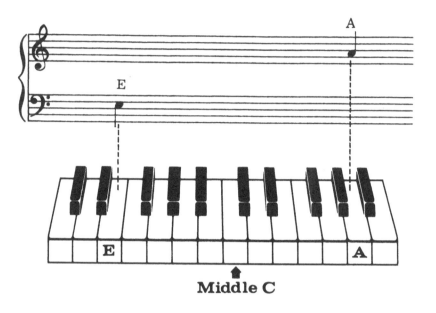

Middle C

DOTTED HALF NOTE

A dot is worth half the value of the note it follows. A DOTTED HALF NOTE (𝅗𝅥.) is held for three counts.

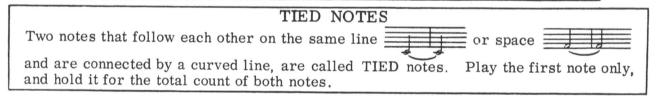

TIED NOTES

Two notes that follow each other on the same line or space and are connected by a curved line, are called TIED notes. Play the first note only, and hold it for the total count of both notes.

Oh How Lovely Is The Evening

French Folk Song

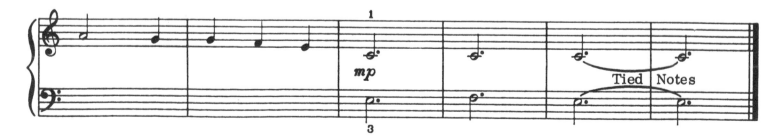

Tied Notes

New Notes

The Interval Of A Fifth

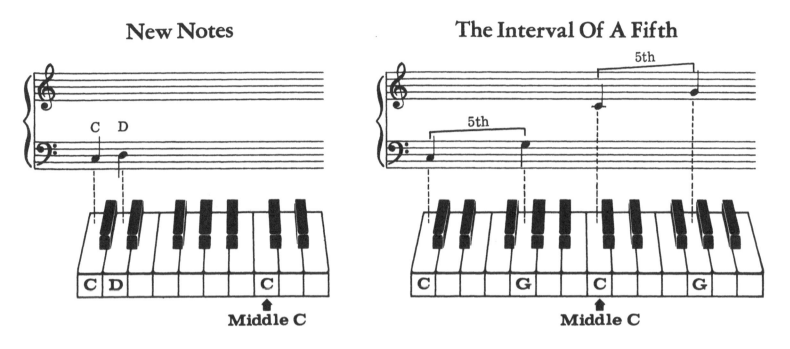

SUGGESTION: In the piece below, find two examples of the Interval of a Fifth.

HELPFUL HINT
Develop the habit of observing the TIME SIGNATURE of each piece before you play it. A good rule is to recite the time signature. For example: this piece is in 3/4 time, which means there are three counts in each measure, and each quarter note gets one count.

Drink To Me Only With Thine Eyes

BEN JONSON

English Melody

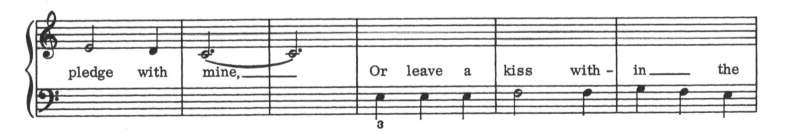

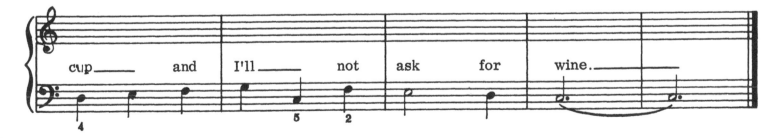

REST SIGNS

A rest sign is used when there are no notes to play in any given measure. It is a period of silence. Each rest gets a certain number of counts, just as notes do.

| Whole Rest | Half Rest | Quarter Rest | Eighth Rest |

STUDENT: On the above staff, draw an example of each rest sign.

VALUE OF THE WHOLE REST

A whole rest is used to indicate a complete measure of silence. The value of a whole rest, therefore, will vary with the time signature. If a time signature reads 2/4, a whole rest will get 2 counts; if it reads 3/4, a whole rest will get 3 counts; if 4/4 it will get four counts.

Blow The Man Down

Sea Chantey

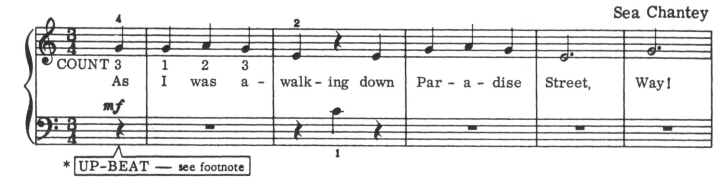

COUNT 3 | 1 2 3 | As I was a - walk-ing down | Par - a - dise | Street, | Way!

* UP-BEAT — see footnote

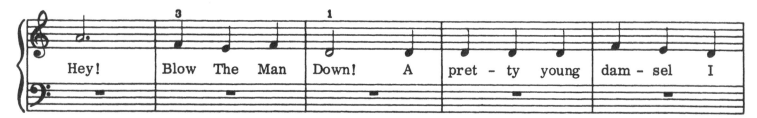

Hey! | Blow The Man Down! | A pret - ty young dam - sel I

chanced for to meet. | Give me some time to Blow The Man Down!

---

* Since this melody starts on the third beat, it is called an UP-BEAT. The first and last measures are incomplete, but when added together, they make one complete measure. Follow the counting directions at the beginning of the piece.

Eighth Notes

♪ This is an eighth note, and has a time value which is half as long as that of a quarter note.

♫ When two eighth notes follow each other, they are connected by a heavy black line. Two such eighth notes have the same value as one quarter note.

SUGGESTED PLAYING PROCEDURE

1. Before playing this piece, clap and count aloud the rhythm of the entire piece. In those measures that have eighth notes, use the word "and" or the syllable "uh" as indicated by the letter *"a"*.

2. Then play and count aloud.

Theme from
Symphony No. 1

JOHANNES BRAHMS
1833 - 1897

---

*This term is called a tempo indication and tells the performer how fast or slow to play a piece (also, sometimes with what kind of feeling). Moderato is Italian meaning "moderate speed". Always look in this spot for the tempo marking and then find the definition in the glossary on page 65.

Home On The Range

Duet

(Teacher's Part)

American Cowboy Song
Arranged by Mark Nevin

Home On The Range

Duet

PUPIL: Play both hands one octave higher than written

American Cowboy Song
Arranged by Mark Nevin

Moderato

Primo

18

The Sharp Sign (♯)

A sharp sign before a note  means to play the nearest key to the right (black or white). It RAISES a note a half step.

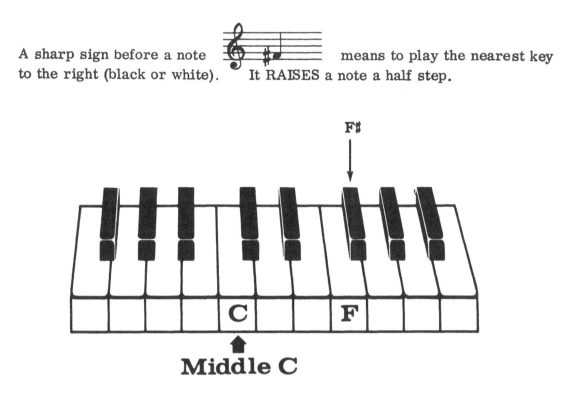

The Flat Sign (♭)

A flat sign before a note  means to play the nearest key to the left (black or white). It LOWERS a note a half step.

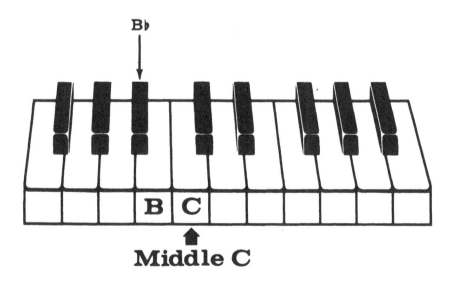

REMEMBER THIS RULE: The Sharp RAISES, the Flat LOWERS.

> ### IMPORTANT RULE
> A sharp or flat placed before any given note will apply only to those notes on the same line or space, in the same measure, and on the same staff.

NOTE: See top of Page 20 for introduction of new notes B and C.

The Lost Chord

ARTHUR SULLIVAN
1842 - 1900
Arranged by Mark Nevin

New Notes

The Interval Of A Sixth

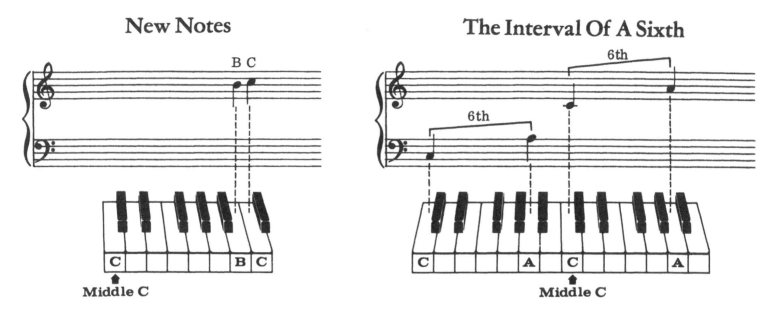

Review These Notes

Note Reading Drill

Write the correct letter name of each note indicated below.

TREBLE

BASS

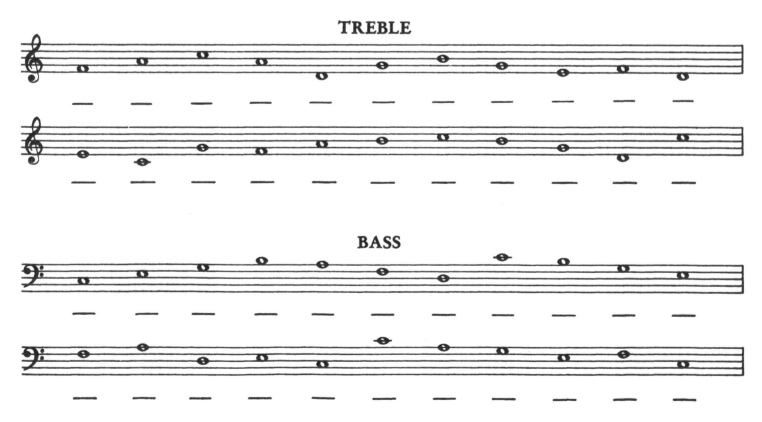

Half Steps
(Semi-Tones)

From any given key to an immediately adjacent key, whether to the right or left (black key or white) is a distance of a HALF STEP or a semi-tone. For example, from C to C♯ (or D♭), or from E to F.

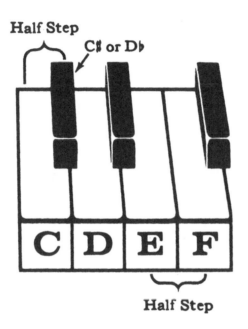

Whole Steps
(Whole Tones)

A whole step consists of two Half Steps. For example, from C to D, C♯ to D♯ (D♭ to E♭), or D to E.

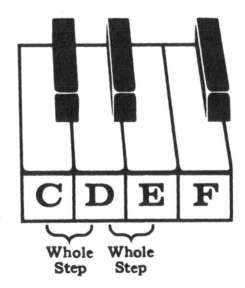

Tetrachords

A TETRACHORD is a segment of a scale consisting of four successive tones; observe the pattern — whole step, whole step, half step.

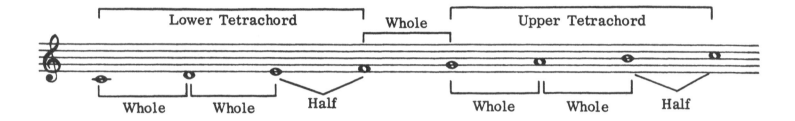

The MAJOR SCALE is made up of TWO TETRACHORDS.

Scale Of C Major

RIGHT HAND

LEFT HAND

NEW MUSICAL SIGNS

Gradually Louder
(*Crescendo*)

Gradually Softer
(*Decrescendo*)

Finger Antics

(A Study In Tetrachords)

MARK NEVIN

Scales Can Be Melodies

Here are two well-known melodies that are based on the Major Scale.

Joy To The World

C MAJOR SCALE (Descending)

The First Noel

C MAJOR SCALE (Ascending)

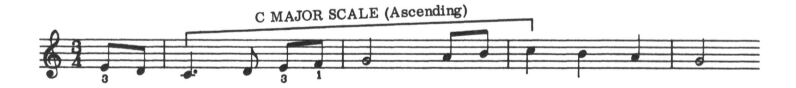

THE DOTTED QUARTER NOTE

On page 12, we learned that a dot adds one half to the value of the note it follows. A dotted $\frac{1}{4}$ note (♩.) is equal to ♩ ♪ ; count the first measure of "The First Noel" as follows:

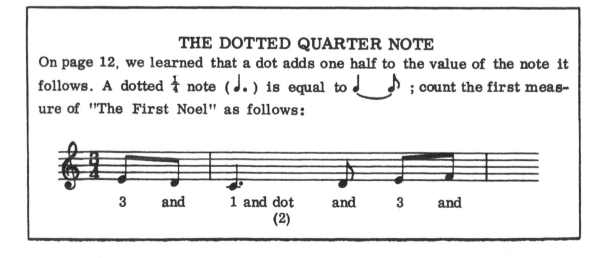

3   and   1 and dot   and   3   and

(2)

Harmonizing The Scale

Play all notes of the following scale 8 keys higher (one octave) than written.

Scale Drill

IMPORTANT: Play this drill several times daily. It will help greatly to develop technique.

The Pedals

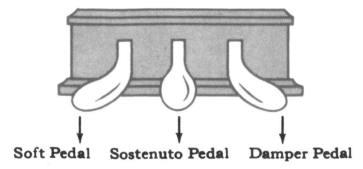

Soft Pedal   Sostenuto Pedal   Damper Pedal

The pedal on the right, which is called the DAMPER PEDAL, is the one most frequently used. It is called the Damper Pedal because, when you press it down, it removes the felt dampers from the strings. Any single tone, or combination of tones, can be sustained by pressing the Damper Pedal.

When the Soft Pedal is pressed down, the strings are muted, thus producing a change in volume of sound as well as quality of tone.

The Sostenuto (sustaining) Pedal is a modification of the damper pedal. It is used to sustain a single note (usually in the bass) or chord. This pedal is rarely used except in advanced stages of piano playing.

Damper Pedal Exercise

STEP 1

Place the right foot on the damper pedal. Follow the counting directions below. Press the pedal DOWN on count 2, let the pedal come UP on count 1. UP on 1, DOWN on 2.

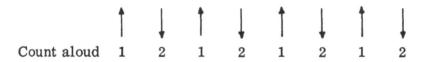

STEP 2

Play each note of the C major scale with the 3rd finger of the R.H. (without pedal). Count aloud as you play. Observe that the sounds from one note to the next are disconnected.

STEP 3

Play the scale again, but this time press the damper pedal DOWN on count 2, and let the pedal come UP on count 1.

Pedal Signs

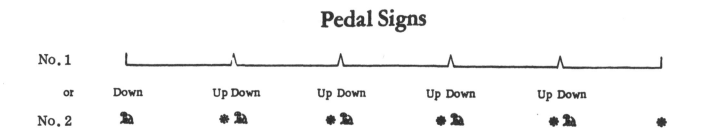

Either of the above signs may be used to indicate when the Damper Pedal is to be used. The sign that is most frequently used, however, is No. 1, showing the straight line with breaks to indicate UP and DOWN movement of the pedal.

Hand Over Hand
(Pedal Study)

MARK NEVIN

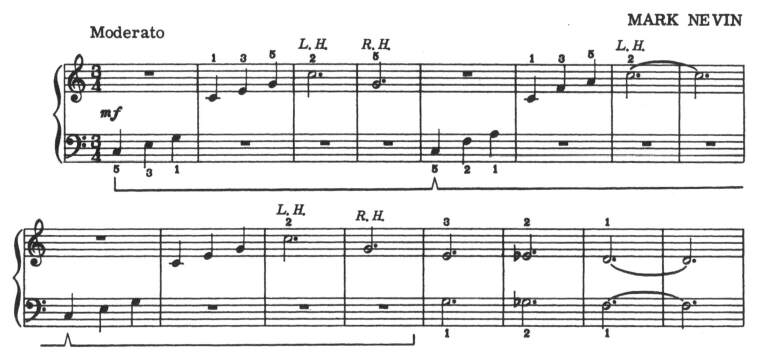

Let's Play Chords

A CHORD consists of the simultaneous sounding of three or more tones.

For example:

3 Tone Chord   4 Tone Chord

Triads

A TRIAD is a chord consisting of three tones. These three tones are the 1st (Root), 3rd and 5th notes of a scale.

For example:

1st
(Root)   3rd   5th

1st   3rd   5th

Played separately (Broken Chord)   Played together

The Three Primary Triads

TONIC   SUB-DOMINANT   DOMINANT

TONIC . . . . I Chord

SUB-DOMINANT . . . . .IV Chord

DOMINANT. . . . . V Chord

ACCENT SIGNS

There are three principal signs used to indicate extra stress on certain notes:

> Light Accent   ∧ Heavy Accent   *sfz – sforzando*
Strong accent on a single
note or chord

Promenade
(Based On The I, IV, V Triads)

MARK NEVIN

New Note D

Inversions

New Notes

E   F   G

A TRIAD may be inverted by changing the order in which the three notes of the Triad appear. A Triad, therefore, has three positions.

Root
Position

First
Inversion

Second
Inversion

Procession
(A Study In Inversions)

MARK NEVIN

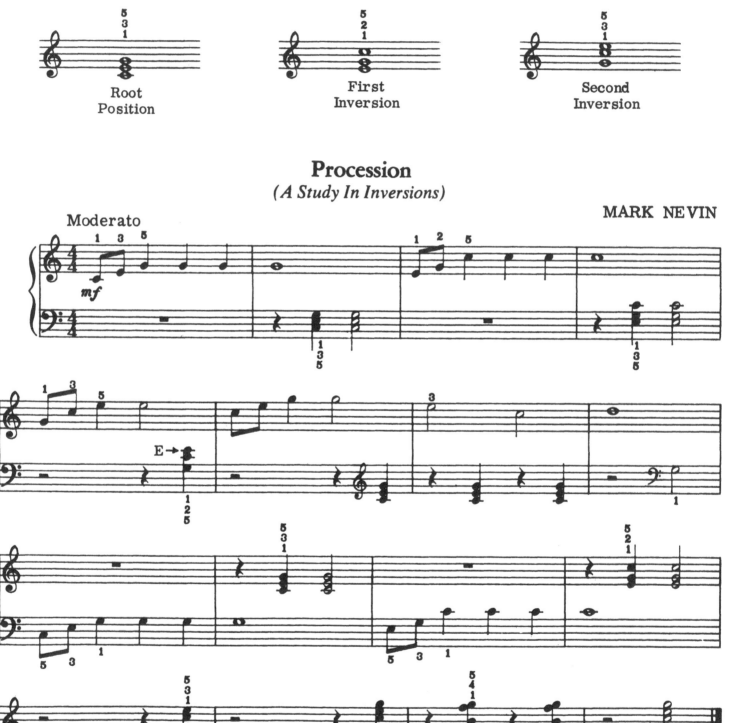

Strolling

MARK NEVIN

NEW MUSICAL TERM

rit. is the abbreviation of the word ritardando, which means "Gradually slower". It is commonly called ritard.

The Slur

The slur is a curved line connecting two or more different notes to show that they are to be played LEGATO, which means "smooth," "connected," "bound together." For example:

The Phrase

Just as in written language, a sentence may be broken down into clauses (or phrases), indicated by punctuation marks, so in music may a melody be broken into phrases, which are indicated by the slur. The most common phrase lengths are two, four or eight measures. As a singer takes a breath at the end of a phrase, so the pianist "takes a breath" at the end of a slur. He does so by raising the hand up from the keys. Observe the phrases indicated by the slurs in "SILHOUETTE."

Silhouette

MARK NEVIN

Andantino

---

*The Natural Sign (♮)

The natural sign is used to cancel a previous sharp or flat.

Technique
(Finger Drill)

> **PRACTICE SUGGESTION**
> Play the following finger drill several times daily. Start at a slow tempo,
> and make each succeeding repetition twice as fast as the previous one.

Key Of G Major

REVIEW page 22 concerning the construction of the Major Scale.

Building The Scale Of G Major

A scale is identified by the name of the first note on which it starts.

STUDENT: Write the missing notes on the staff below to complete the Scale of G major.

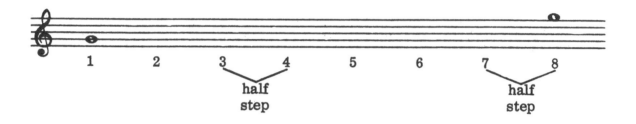

Observe that the 7th note, F, has to be sharped in order to have a half step between the 7th and 8th notes. We can conclude, therefore, that the SIGNATURE OF THE KEY OF G major is one sharp—F♯.

Key Signature

The Three Principal Chords Of The Key Of G Major

Alma Mater

College Song
Arranged by Mark Nevin

Staccato Touch

STACCATO means "disconnected" or "detached," the opposite of LEGATO, which is "smooth" or "connected." When a note is to be played staccato, it is indicated by a dot over (𝅘𝅥) or under (𝅘𝅥) the note. The staccato touch is accomplished by a quick release of the finger from the key.

NEW MUSICAL TERMS

In the last measure of "Contrasts," you will see the terms "D. C. (Da Capo) al Fine." This means return to the beginning of the piece and play again until you come to the measure with the word "Fine" (pronounced fee-nay), which means "end."

Contrasts
(A Study In Staccato And Legato)

MARK NEVIN

D. C. al Fine

The Mimic

DMITRI KABALEVSKY
1904 -

Intervals Of 2nds, 3rds, 5ths

Instant Recognition Of The Interval Of A 2nd

Notice that in the interval of a 2nd (harmonic), the note-heads always assume a "side-by-side" position.

All Intervals are either HARMONIC or MELODIC.

Harmonic Intervals

When two tones are sounded together, it is called a HARMONIC INTERVAL.

Melodic Intervals

When two tones are sounded after each other, it is called a MELODIC INTERVAL.

Interval Drill

2nds, 3rds and 5ths

STUDENT: Using whole notes, write the missing note required for each of the following intervals. The first interval is done as an example.

Harmonic Intervals

| 3rd | 2nd above | 5th below | 3rd above | 2nd below | 5th above | 3rd below | 2nd above |

Melodic Intervals

The first interval is done as an example.

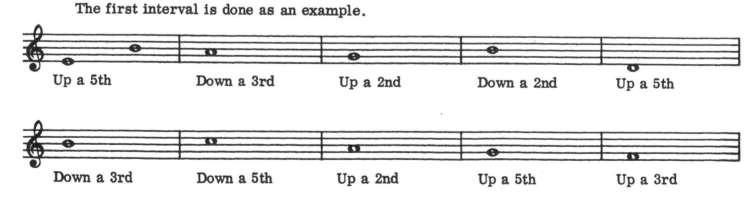

| Up a 5th | Down a 3rd | Up a 2nd | Down a 2nd | Up a 5th |

| Down a 3rd | Down a 5th | Up a 2nd | Up a 5th | Up a 3rd |

NEW NOTE D

HELPFUL HINT

Before you play this piece, examine the notes of the Left Hand, and identify all the Harmonic Intervals of 2nds and 3rds. Examine the notes of the Right Hand, and identify all the Melodic Intervals of 2nds and 3rds.

I'm Called Little Buttercup

(from "H.M.S. Pinafore")

GILBERT and SULLIVAN
Arranged by Mark Nevin

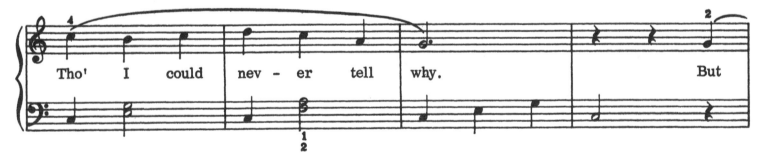

Interval Drill

4ths, 6ths and 7ths

STUDENT: Using whole notes, write the missing note required for each of the following intervals. The first interval is done as an example.

Harmonic Intervals

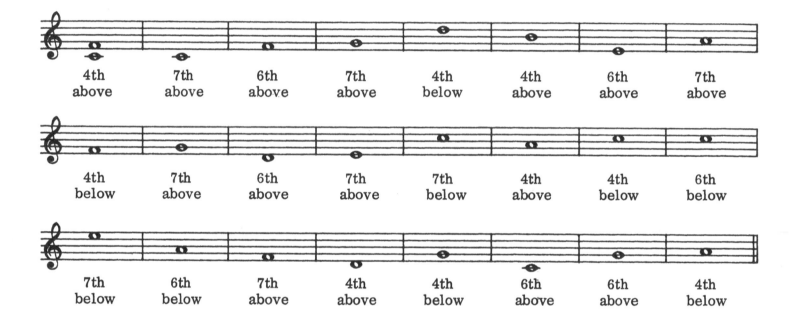

| 4th above | 7th above | 6th above | 7th above | 4th below | 4th above | 6th above | 7th above |

| 4th below | 7th above | 6th above | 7th above | 7th below | 4th above | 4th below | 6th below |

| 7th below | 6th below | 7th above | 4th above | 4th below | 6th above | 6th above | 4th below |

Melodic Intervals

The first interval is done as an example.

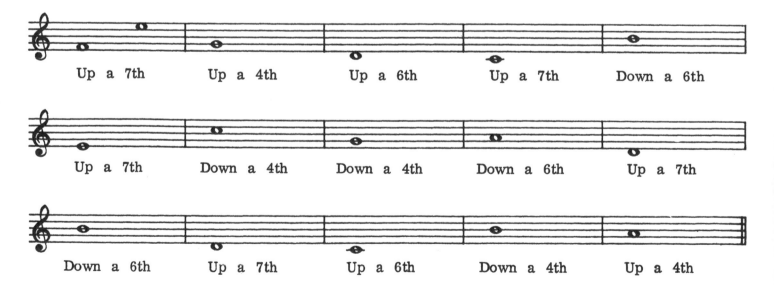

| Up a 7th | Up a 4th | Up a 6th | Up a 7th | Down a 6th |

| Up a 7th | Down a 4th | Down a 4th | Down a 6th | Up a 7th |

| Down a 6th | Up a 7th | Up a 6th | Down a 4th | Up a 4th |

NEW MUSICAL TERMS

poco a poco dim. (diminuendo) — little by little get softer

Theme from the
Sixth Symphony

PETER ILYITCH TCHAIKOVSKY
1840 - 1893
Adapted and Arranged by
Mark Nevin

Andante (Slow)

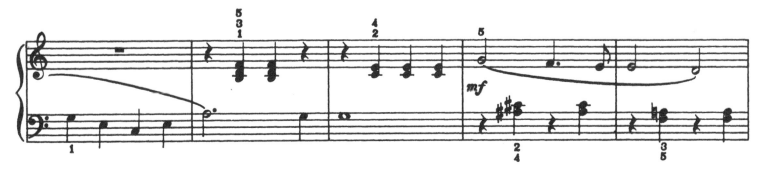

poco a poco dim.

Six-Eight Time

This time signature means there are SIX COUNTS to each measure, and each eighth note gets ONE count. Study the note values below for 6/8 time.

♪ — 1 count

♩ — 2 counts

♩. — 3 counts

𝅗𝅥. — 6 counts

Here's a melody in 6/8 time. Count aloud as you play it.

1 2 3 4 5 6   1 2 3 4 5 6   1 2 3 4 5 6   1 2 3 4 5 6

Jig

Irish Melody
Arranged by Mark Nevin

Lively

Theme from
Liebestraum
(Excerpt)

FRANZ LISZT
1811 - 1886
Arranged by Mark Nevin

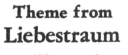

Key Of F Major

Building The Scale Of F Major

STUDENT: Write the missing notes on the staff below to complete the scale of F major.

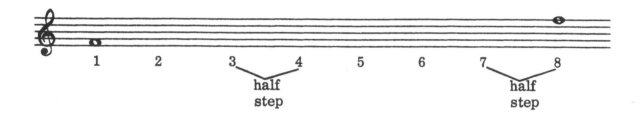

Observe that the 4th note (B) of the scale had to be flatted in order to have a half step between the 3rd and 4th notes.

Key Signature

We can conclude, therefore, that the SIGNATURE OF THE KEY OF F Major is one flat — Bb.

The Three Principal Chords Of The Key Of F Major

REPEAT SIGN

The Repeat Sign calls for the repetition of all measures enclosed by the sign. If the sign appears alone, as in measure 8, the repetition starts from the beginning.

Minuet In F

LEOPOLD MOZART
1719 - 1787
(Father of Wolfgang Amadeus Mozart)
Simplified Arrangement by Mark Nevin

Song Of The Islands

(Na Lei O Hawaii)

CHARLES E. KING
Arranged by Mark Nevin

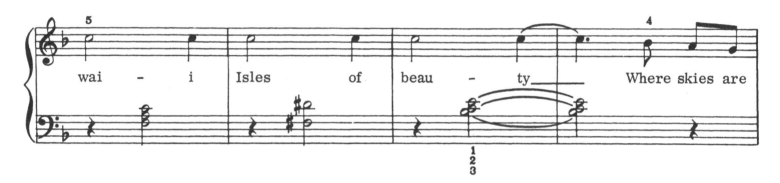

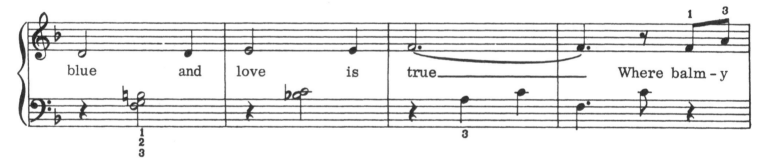

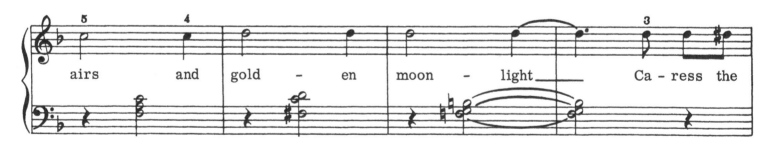

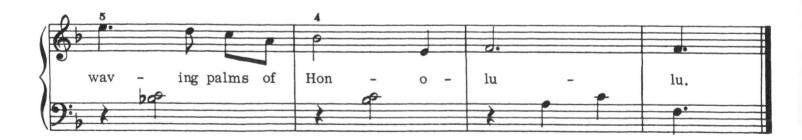

Technique
(Finger Drill)

> **PRACTICE SUGGESTION**
> Play the following finger drill several times daily. Start at a slow tempo, and make each succeeding repetition twice as fast as the previous one.

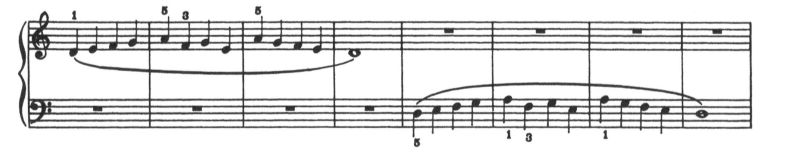

Minor Scales And Keys

Any major scale may be changed to minor by lowering the 3rd and 6th notes of the major scale a half step. For example:

Scale Of C Major

Scale Of C Minor
*(Harmonic Form)**

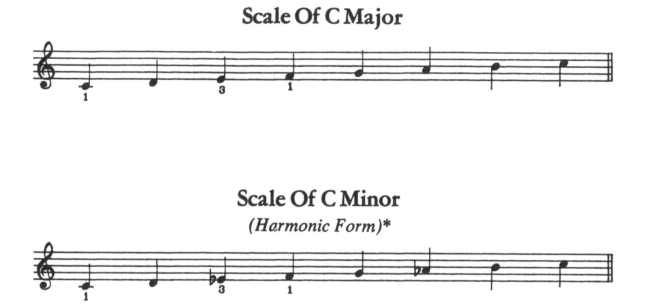

Compare the whole step/half step relationships of the minor scales with what you have already learned about the major scales (page 22).

Parallel Minor

The above scale of C minor is called the Parallel Minor of C major, because the letter names of both scales are the same. Observe the difference between the PARALLEL MINOR relationship and the RELATIVE MINOR relationship, which is explained on the next page.

---

*There are three forms of the minor scale, NATURAL, HARMONIC, MELODIC. See next page for examples.

Relative Minor

The Relative Minor of any given major key is always found on the 6th degree (note) of the major scale. For example:

Scale Of C Major

6th degree

Scale Of A Minor

(Relative Minor Of C Major)

NATURAL FORM

HARMONIC FORM (Raised 7th)

MELODIC FORM (Raised 6th and 7th ascending, then lowered descending.)

How To Change Major Triads To Minor

Any Major triad may be changed to minor by lowering the 3rd of the triad a half step. For example:

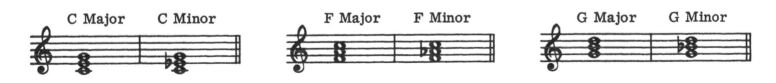

C Major   C Minor   F Major   F Minor   G Major   G Minor

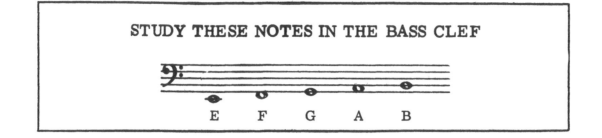

STUDY THESE NOTES IN THE BASS CLEF

Theme from the
Symphony No. 7
(Key Of A Minor)

LUDWIG VAN BEETHOVEN
1770 - 1827
Arranged by Mark Nevin

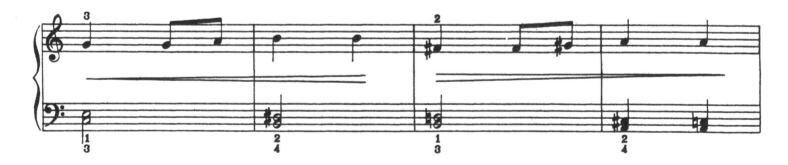

NEW MUSICAL TERMS

Two new terms appear on this page — "Op." (abbreviation for the word Opus), and "a tempo." All terms are defined on page 65.

HELPFUL HINT

Be sure to play the right hand softly throughout, and emphasize the melody in the left hand.

Melody For The Left Hand

Waltz In A Minor
Op. 34, No. 2
(Excerpt)

FREDERIC CHOPIN
1810 - 1849
Arranged by Mark Nevin

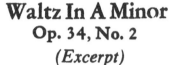

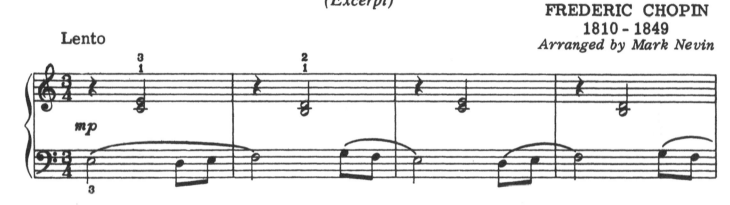

Leger Lines

LEGER LINES are the added lines used for notes written above or below the five lines of the staff (Treble or Bass). See examples below:

German Dance
(Excerpt)

LUDWIG VAN BEETHOVEN
1770 - 1827

Preparatory Chord Study For The Left Hand

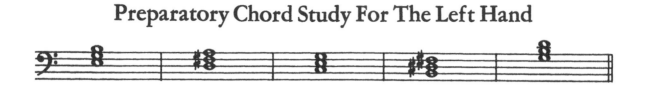

Greensleeves

Key of E minor, related to G major

English Air
Arranged by Mark Nevin

The Dominant Seventh Chord

A Dominant Triad is always built on the 5th degree of the scale. For example, in the key of C major:

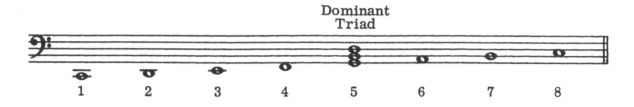

The Dominant Triad plus an interval of a 7th (g to f), will form a DOMINANT SEVENTH CHORD. The symbol for this chord is V7.

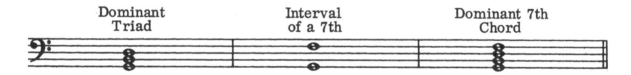

Since the Dominant 7th Chord consists of 4 notes (g-b-d-f), it has 3 inversions.

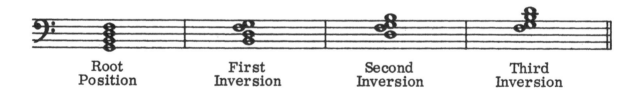

The First Inversion of the Dominant 7th Chord very often appears with one note (the 5th) omitted.

For example:

NEW NOTE E

NEW MUSICAL SIGN

C This sign, used in the time signature, stands for 4/4 time, and is also called "Common Time."

Yellow Rose Of Texas

American Folk Tune
Arranged by Mark Nevin

There's a yel-low rose in Tex-as I'm go-ing back to see, No

oth - er fel - low knows her, no fel - low, on - ly me; She

cried so when I left her, It like to break my heart, And

if I ev - er find her, we nev - er more will part.

Dominant 7th Chord

Arpeggios

The word ARPEGGIO is borrowed from the Italian, and it means "harp–like." When the tones of a chord are played in rapid, even succession (and extended into one or more octaves), it is called an ARPEGGIO.

For example:

Following is an arpeggio based on the C major triad, to be played alternately between right and left hands. Notes with stems down ⌐ are to be played by the Left Hand; notes with stems up ⌐ are to be played by the Right Hand. (Note: This direction applies only to the following exercise.)

The Harpist
(Arpeggio Study)

MARK NEVIN

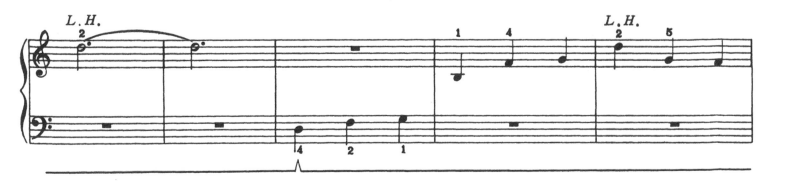

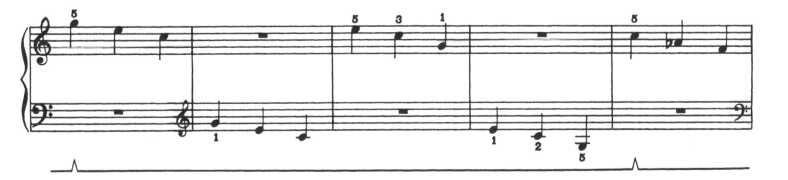

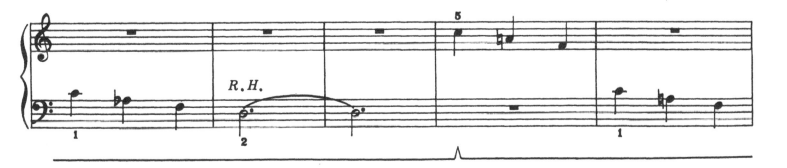

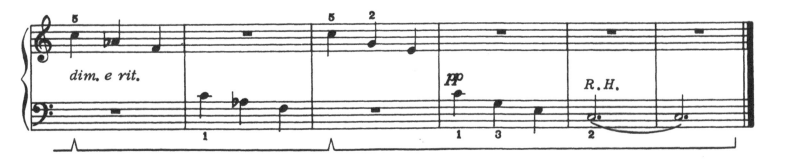

Key Of D Major

Building The Scale Of D Major

STUDENT: Write the missing notes on the staff below to complete the scale of D major.

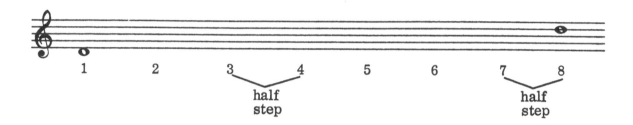

1   2   3   4   5   6   7   8

half step   half step

Observe that the two notes (f and c) of the scale, had to be sharped in order to provide a half step between the 3rd and 4th notes, and the 7th and 8th notes.

Key Signature

We can conclude, therefore, that the SIGNATURE OF THE KEY OF D major is two sharps— F♯ and C♯.

The Three Principal Chords Of The Key Of D Major

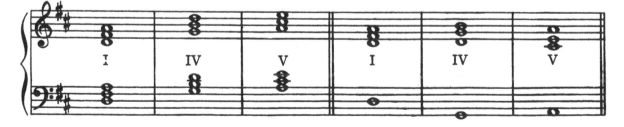

I   IV   V   I   IV   V

American Patrol

F. W. MEACHAM
Arranged by Mark Nevin

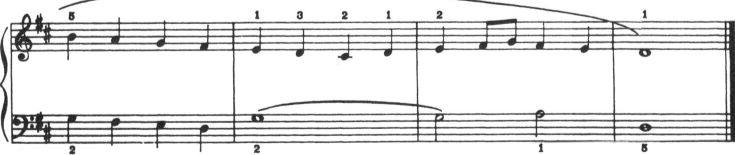

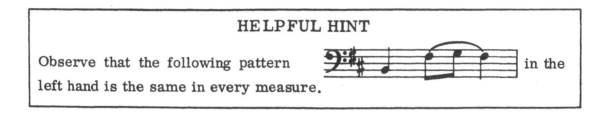

HELPFUL HINT

Observe that the following pattern in the left hand is the same in every measure.

Tum-Balalaika

Key of B minor, related to D major

Russian Folk Song
Arranged by Mark Nevin

Allegretto

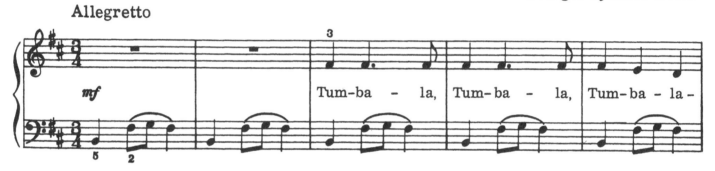

Preparatory Chord Study For The Left Hand

Theme from the
Polovtsian Dances
(From the Opera "Prince Igor")
Key of D minor, related to F major

ALEXANDER BORODIN
1833 - 1887
Arranged by Mark Nevin

Summary Of Scales*, Chords And Triads
Used In This Book

C Major

A Minor

G Major

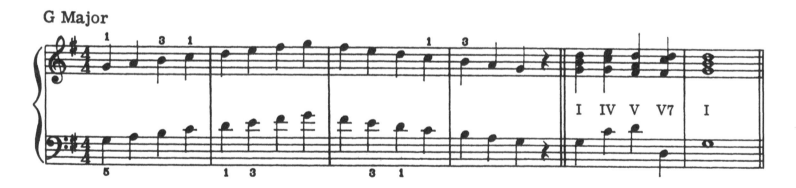

E Minor

*The minor scales that appear on this page and the next are shown in the Harmonic form only.

D Major

B Minor

F Major

D Minor

NOTE TO TEACHER

The student who has successfully completed this book, is ready to progress to BOOK TWO of PIANO FOR ADULTS by Mark Nevin.

Test Yourself
NOTE READING AND WRITING

Write the correct letter name for each note.

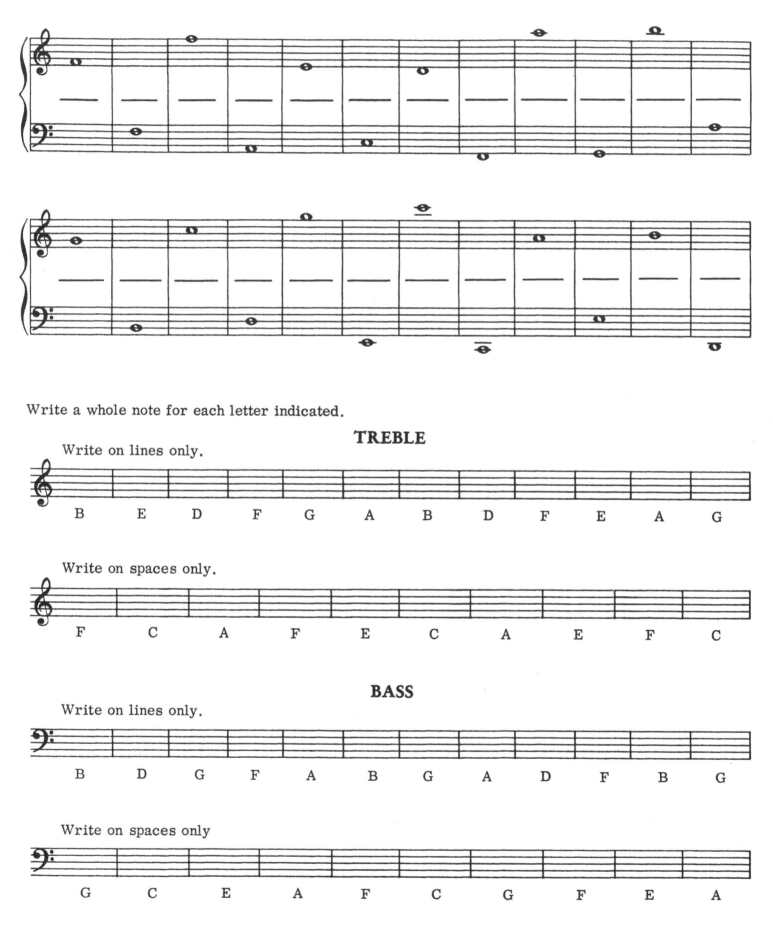

Write a whole note for each letter indicated.

TREBLE

Write on lines only.

B E D F G A B D F E A G

Write on spaces only.

F C A F E C A E F C

BASS

Write on lines only.

B D G F A B G A D F B G

Write on spaces only

G C E A F C G F E A